AN ABBEVILLE ANTHOLOGY

MOTHER

— AND —

DAUGHTER

TALES

For my daughter, Rachel
J. E.-S.

First published in Great Britain in 1996 by Barefoot Books Ltd.

First published in the United States of America in 1996 by Abbeville Press,

22 Cortlandt Street, New York, N.Y. 10007.

This book has been printed on 100% acid-free paper

Printed and bound in Hong Kong

First edition

10 9 8 7 6 5 4 3 2

ISBN 0-7892-0281-6

An Abbeville Anthology

MOTHER

— AND —

DAUGHTER

TALES

Retold by Josephine Evetts-Secker

Illustrated by Helen Cann

ABBEVILLE KIDS

A Division of Abbeville Publishing Group

New York   London   Paris

CONTENTS

FOREWORD

These stories are about mothers, grandmothers, stepmothers, god-mothers, foster mothers, and mothers-in-law as they weave their mysterious relationships with their maturing daughters.

The tales come from many different cultures; but each gives us vivid images of being a daughter and a mother, with the blessings and contradictions experienced in being either, or both. When the bond between mother and daughter is strong and the mother has been an effective role model, then the daughter can experience her mother within herself as an inner strength. This is the effect of the good mother in many stories, where the mother gives something of herself to her child before death. For mothers must "die" and daughters must be prepared to leave the protection of home and to be alone.

Every daughter must have an adventure; she needs to create her own story to become her own person. No matter how much mothers, anxious for their daughters' safety or success, insist that they "go straight" to their destination, daughters must always take their own circuitous route, and mothers can only watch and suffer, or watch and rejoice.

These tales are never afraid of life as it is; they tackle directly such emotions as jealousy, hatred, and cruelty, suggesting that they are a part of life; they must be owned, not wished away. And we must sometimes enter the murky depths of our own forests to encounter the devouring energy of the paradoxical Baba Yaga, who is both devouring and creative. Death is ground for life and renewal, most vividly enacted in the myth of Persephone.

The tales I have gathered here are about preparation and readiness for union with and unity within the cosmos. This is what falling in love in fairy tales evokes, and their narratives guide, compel, or drag us towards integration. These daughters seek union and community as vibrant and increasingly autonomous young women, who can lie, disobey, love, and create, in whatever ways are necessary to foster life. They must often suffer an enforced isolation which becomes a time of incubation; for inwardness must balance extraverted action.

The stories can be ascribed to no originating author. For centuries they have been told and retold within and across national boundaries. They appear in many forms, suggesting that certain ideas and experiences are universal. Knowledge of these tales helps us to create meaningful experience out of the inadvertent happenings of our lives, and to see pattern in randomness. In my retellings, I have tried to maintain the universal qualities of myth and folk/fairy tale, while allowing for local color and custom, as we move from country to country, with all their varieties of social order, religious belief, and geography. I have tried, wherever possible, to be faithful to the earliest records I found, while remaining open to the many individual versions I have read or heard.

These stories live by "endless mutation." A Native American tale claims that the source of story is the "story-telling stone," which says to its first listeners, "Some of you will remember every word I say, some will remember a part of the words, and surely some will forget them all. Hereafter, you must tell these stories to each other … you must keep them for as long as the world lasts." This collection hopes to obey that stone's imperative.

Josephine Evetts-Secker

Calgary, Alberta 1996

DEMETER AND PERSEPHONE

GREEK

Demeter, the stately goddess of nature, stood at the edge of the meadow watching her beautiful daughter play with the nymphs of the pools and streams. "She will be safe and happy here among the flowers until I return from Mount Olympus," thought Demeter. So she shook her golden hair and left her child with the hyacinth, crocus, and iris that flowered all the year round. Persephone waved goodbye to her mother and watched her tall figure grow smaller as she went off on her errand. Soon she had disappeared.

Persephone immediately looked around her. She could scarcely see her friends in the high grasses, though she could hear them laugh and splash as they dived into the pool. She had played in these fields for as long as she could remember. Until this moment she had delighted in sun-filled days of hide and seek and races. But now she felt strangely discontented and searched for something new to interest her.

In the distance she caught sight of clusters of white flowers. "Ah, the narcissus," she murmured. "I must gather some of them for Mother when she returns." She ran off to the tree-shaded spot where they grew and reached out eagerly to pick the first flower. But the stalk did not snap as easily as she had expected, so she pulled harder. Still the flower did not break free. Persephone tugged and strained. "How deep these roots must be," she thought. "They must reach right down beneath the earth!" Suddenly, the plant came free in her hand and she saw that the whole root had been pulled out of the soil, leaving a gaping hole. She was intrigued by this and sat down, gazing curiously into the disturbed black soil.

Deep down in the Shades below, King Hades, Lord of the Underworld, felt his kingdom jolt. Quickly he yoked his gleaming black stallions to his chariot and rode to the surface, checking the crust of the earth for cracks that might let the daylight into his gloomy realm. The tremors of earthquakes terrified him: he must always be alert.

King Hades rose up to the fragrant meadow to investigate, and there he saw the young goddess Persephone. In that moment his heart was struck by the arrow of the irresistible love-god, Eros. As soon as King Hades felt these pangs of love, he seized the startled girl and prepared to carry her off in his shining chariot down into his dark kingdom.

"Help me! Help! Mother! Anybody … help me!" Persephone cried into the still air. But only the speechless waters heard her calls. As she struggled,

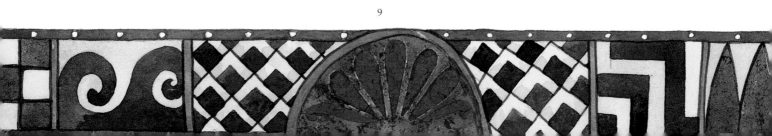

her belt fell from her and dropped with a splash into the ruffled pool where she and the nymphs had been bathing.

When Demeter returned some hours later, she was horrified to find her daughter's girdle floating on the surface of the pool, and her heart froze with fear. Persephone's companions had fled in fright and no one remained to tell what had happened to her dearest child. So her search began.

Demeter's heart pounded as she ran through the fields calling out her daughter's special name: "Kore! Kore!" Frantic with fear, she tore at her long hair and raced here and there like a madwoman. Some say the river nymphs finally told her what had happened—that her child was not dead but snatched away by the Lord of the Underworld. Others say that it was the sun who told her that Persephone was now the bride of the noble God of Death and queen of his kingdom.

Hearing this, Demeter raged and wept and withdrew all her love and care from the earth. She stopped the rain from falling; she let the hot sun burn down on dry dust; she broke up the plows and kicked over the barren furrows. The farmers and their families grew weak for lack of food. All the people of the earth were bewildered and filled with fear. They called on the great goddess with the golden hair, who had always been their friend; but they no longer found her swaying with the grain in the gentle winds. For Demeter now had only one thought, vengeance; and only one feeling, pain.

"If Persephone cannot live with me," the powerful earth mother threatened, "then without her nothing will be left to live."

The mighty god Zeus sat on Olympus, mountain of the gods, and watched with alarm as Demeter destroyed the earth. People offered sacrifices and pleaded for his help. "Great Zeus, save us from famine and death!" they cried. But the soil became barren and suffering covered the earth like a cold fog.

Then in her rage Demeter stormed high Olympus, demanding that mighty Zeus use his matchless power to bring back their daughter from the Underworld. "Bring back our child, my Kore," she screamed, in a voice that rivalled Zeus' own thunder.

Zeus tried to comfort Demeter, saying, "I have heard from a river nymph that our child is now a queen, reigning with dignity in her new kingdom."

Demeter would not be comforted, crying even more wildly, "Bring her back to me, or I will let all things die!"

At last Zeus realized that if life was to continue on earth, he must give in to her demand. Wearily he relented, "If Persephone has not eaten anything in the dark realm, the Lord of the Underworld must return her to you," he commanded. "I will send the winged god Hermes with that message to my terrible and gloomy brother, King Hades."

Hermes approached the throne of Zeus to be told his errand. "You must make your way down from Olympus to the Underworld with all speed," Zeus commanded, "and demand the release of Persephone. Our brother will be reluctant to let her go, but you must insist that this is the will of Zeus." As Hermes turned to depart, Zeus called after him, "But, of course, if Persephone has eaten anything in the Underworld, then she must stay there, for she will have accepted Hades' provision. That is the custom."

Demeter was weak from despair and hunger, for she herself had not touched one crumb of food since her search began, and she had drunk only a few cups of water and barley-meal. She knew that Persephone would be

pining for her mother, just as she pined for her child.

But in the dim land where Persephone now reigned, the young goddess, while resisting all other food, had been tempted by the luscious red fruit of the pomegranate that grew in the midst of Hades' misty garden. She had eaten only seven single seeds, but the red juice of each one had spilled on her white garment as she crushed them between her teeth.

Persephone rejoiced when she heard Zeus' message that she could have safe and immediate passage back to her mother's embrace. But her heart sank at Hermes' next words: "Persephone, I will take you home, but first I must know whether you have eaten anything while you have been in this realm."

The young girl remembered the bright sweet fruit and replied, "Oh yes, I have eaten of Hades' fruit, but only a few tiny seeds."

Hermes had no choice but to dash her hopes: "Then you must remain here. It is the will of Zeus." At this Persephone broke down, weeping for the light and the flowers and her mother's fierce love.

Wise Zeus surveyed the scene before him: in the Underworld, a grieving daughter and a determined husband; on the earth, a raging mother, and multitudes of people starved and dying. The sounds of mourning and wailing filled the ears of the god. How were the fruits of the earth to be revived? How could he appease the other gods? He pondered the problem from his throne on the high mountain. Then he proclaimed his solution— a wise decree.

"The noble young goddess Persephone will stay with her dark husband for a part of every year. My brother Hades needs a queen and his gloomy realm needs to be brightened by love. But at a certain time each year Persephone will rise from beneath the earth and join her mother. Persephone is the golden corn-maiden, so it is fair that she should spend part of the year with her mother, the goddess of the earth and all that grows there."

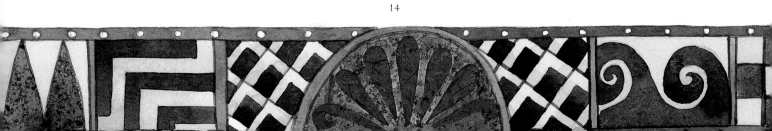

And so it happens that every spring Persephone returns to Demeter. Together they rejoice at the seeding of corn, the growth of green leaves and the ripening of the yellow grain. The young goddess wanders with the nymphs again. They pick flowers and bind red poppies in their hair as they have always done. But after the harvest has been gathered and the grain is safely stored in the farmers' silos, the young queen is called back down to the Underworld, where King Hades is yearning for her return. She descends to her dark husband and lives with him through the long winter months. During this time, it is as though nothing grows in the earth, for the life of next year's plants is hidden deep beneath the soil. Frosts come, snows fall, and all is still as Demeter waits silently for her daughter to return. Then, Persephone begins to feel once again the pull of greenness and light. Quickly, she springs to life and moves up through the rich, black soil to the earth's crust, breaking through it into the arms of the great earth mother, Demeter.

Every year Persephone divides her time between the earth and the Underworld. So life is constantly renewed, and the wintry grip of Hades is overthrown.

THE WATERFALL OF
WHITE HAIR

CHINESE

Once upon a time in China there lived a girl with the longest hair you have ever seen. It was shining and black and reached past her ankles. She had to tie it up so that it didn't drag along the ground. Everyone called her Long Hair.

Long Hair lived with her mother, who was old and weak, so the girl had to take care of her, doing all the housework and feeding the pigs. Since there was no stream nearby, she had to fetch water from far away, along with all the other villagers. Each morning as she trudged along with the heavy water jar, she thought how strange it was that there were no streams rushing down from Lofty Mountain above their village. But the mountain was dry. Long

Hair fetched water through the heat of the summer and the cold days of winter, and she never complained.

One day, Long Hair took a walk up the mountain and found she was climbing higher than usual. When she stopped to rest, she found a strange, leafy plant that she had never seen before. Thinking that her pigs would enjoy it, she pulled the plant out of the ground to take it home. To her surprise, a huge, round radish came out in her hands, and out of the hole it had made in the ground rushed a stream of sparkling water.

"This is such good water," she thought as she drank her fill, and she sank back in contentment on the grass. Suddenly, a sharp wind arose, snatched the radish out of her hand, and dropped it back into its hole. The water stopped instantly. The wind went on blowing and buffeted Long Hair from place to place, until she took shelter behind some rocks, and found herself in the presence of an old man with golden hair.

"You have discovered my secret!" he shouted angrily. "You must never, ever, speak of it to anyone, or you will die. I am the Spirit of Lofty Mountain—this secret water is mine!" Before Long Hair could reply, she was tossed back to her own garden.

She remained silent that day as she went about her work. In the weeks that followed, her heart grew heavy, for she began to see how difficult life was for her people. She grew sadder and sadder as she watched the weary villagers, including the old and the weak and the very young, as they toiled home along the dry and stony road with their heavy loads of water from the faraway stream. Long Hair had never before noticed what a burden this was. But now her sorrow swelled and her hair began to turn grey. Then it grew

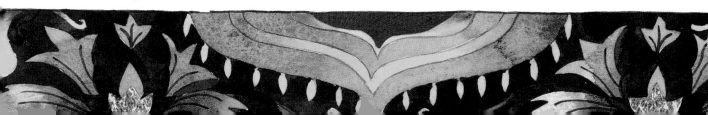

white, until it was as white as freshly fallen snow. And still Long Hair worried, knowing that she could make it easier for the villagers to fetch water.

One morning, as she walked sadly along the road, Long Hair saw an old woman struggling with her water jars. The woman could hardly lift the jars, let alone carry them. All of a sudden, she collapsed on the road and cut her head on a sharp stone. Her precious water spilled over the thirsty ground and was lost at once. As she helped the woman to her feet, Long Hair's heart flashed with anger and she decided to spurn the Mountain Spirit's warning. Calling all the people to follow her up the mountain, she announced, "There is plenty of water close by. It is ours too—Lofty Mountain must share it with us."

Soon the villagers reached the spot high up where the strange radish plant grew. Once again, Long Hair pulled at its big leaves and the radish came out of the earth, leaving the hole through which the stream of water flowed. Everyone was delighted and thanked Long Hair again and again. "We must chop the radish to pieces," she instructed them, "so that it can never again dam up our stream." When this was done, the cold water flowed faster and faster, and the people splashed and drank and rejoiced.

Suddenly, the wind began to gather on the mountain, and Long Hair remembered the words of the Mountain Spirit. As she did so, she was whisked away by the turbulent wind, which brought her again to the yellow-haired old man in his rock shelter. His face was even angrier than before and he shouted, "Evil girl! You have betrayed my secret and you must be punished. You will lie forever over the rocky side of my mountain where the stream rushes out of the shallow earth, and the freezing cold waters will race over you, pouring down through your long white hair. This is your punishment!"

Long Hair shivered at the very thought, but she said bravely, "So be it. If that brings water to my people, I shall endure it. But please, O Spirit of Lofty Mountain, let me first go back to my mother to say goodbye and to find someone to take care of her when I am gone."

The Spirit groaned, for he was not used to saying yes to anyone. But in spite of himself, he was touched by the girl's request, so he said reluctantly, "You may go, but you must return before nightfall, or everyone will suffer."

The wind again howled, blowing Long Hair back to her own village, where the happy people had already begun to celebrate. Her heart grieved as she said goodbye to her pigs, and it nearly broke when she parted from her mother, knowing that she would never see her again, but not breathing a word of this for fear of upsetting her even more.

She went into the garden and stood weeping beneath her favorite tree, where she had so often rested. Suddenly, a man with green hair appeared out of the tree and spoke to her kindly. "Dear girl, wipe away your tears. I will help you, for you are generous and your heart is kind. I have carved a likeness of you in stone. It is a good likeness, but if we are to fool the Mountain Spirit into believing that it is really you, you must sacrifice your long white hair."

Without a moment's hesitation, Long Hair let the man cut off her hair and attach it to the head of the stone statue. Now Lofty Mountain would think the statue was Long Hair herself.

This time the wind blew more fiercely than ever, carrying Long Hair with the green man and the statue back up the mountain. Together they laid the statue face down, so that the long white hair hung over the

precipice. The water then flowed through the hair, forming a beautiful cascade of sparkling water over which rainbows played.

Now the wind took Long Hair up again and dropped her back beneath her favorite tree. The green-haired man was no longer there, but his voice spoke from the tree, saying, "Long Hair, you are kind and loving. Return to your mother for she needs you. Return to your friends and your village, where you will always be remembered for your kindness and courage. Live there in peace for as long as the waterfall tumbles down Lofty Mountain."

So Long Hair went back to her mother and they lived peacefully for many years. Soon her own head began to grow hair again, black and gleaming as it was before. And to this day the grateful villagers look up in thanks at the mountain and watch the glorious Waterfall of White Hair racing down to supply them with water.

MOTHER HOLLE

GERMAN

There was once a widow who had raised two girls, one her own daughter and the other her stepdaughter. She was devoted to her own child, even though the girl was selfish and lazy. The stepdaughter was hated by both mother and sister, even though she was generous and always willing to help. She was made to work from dawn till dark, and the silly girl never complained.

Every day she was forced to spend hours spinning, so she would take her work to the well beside the road, where she could watch the world go by. There she would sit and spin till her fingers bled, hoping to satisfy her step-mother. But it was impossible, for the more she worked, the more the unkind woman demanded of her.

Then one day, as she sat spinning harder than ever, the blood on her fingers made the spindle sticky. So she leaned over the well-side to wash it, as she

often did. But the spindle dropped out of her hand and fell down into the dark water. She cried out in dismay, "Oh, what shall I do?" for she knew that her stepmother would be angry. Indeed, when the cruel woman heard what had happened, she scolded her loudly and ordered her to go down the well to get the spindle back. "Don't you dare come home without it!" she screamed.

With a heavy heart the girl returned to the well. Bending over the side, she was surprised to see her own beautiful reflection on the surface of the water, disturbed only by the splashes made by her tears. As the water beckoned to her, in she jumped. She closed her eyes and gasped as she plunged to the bottom of the well. When she opened them again, she could see blue sky above and green grass all around. The sun shone brightly on flowers of many colors.

She jumped up and ran happily across to the other side of the meadow. There she found a large oven, smelling of freshly baked bread, and heard voices calling, "Take us out! Oh, please take us out, or else we will burn. We have been baking long enough!" So she did as the bread asked, carefully removing each loaf from the hot oven and setting it down to cool. Satisfied, she walked on.

After a while, she heard more voices calling out urgently, "Pick us! Oh, please pick us, or we will become too ripe!" She looked around and saw a huge tree, bent to the ground with the weight of the round, red apples hanging from its branches. So she shook the tree till the apples began to drop. She shook the tree and she shook it again, till every apple had fallen, covering the ground in a rich, ruddy carpet. The apples were scattered far and wide by the shaking, so she gathered them together and left them in a heap beneath the tree.

Tired and hungry, she walked on even farther, till she came to a strange-

looking cottage. She stopped dead in her tracks when she saw the face of an old woman spying out of the window. At the sight of the old crone's huge teeth, she drew back in terror. But the old woman hobbled out of the house towards her, beckoning to her, and calling so kindly that she came closer.

"Do not be afraid, dear child," said the old woman. "Come in and visit. If you will stay with me and help me every day, you will be very happy."

The girl whispered in response, "What must I do for you?"

Smiling, the old woman replied, "You must take care of the whole house.

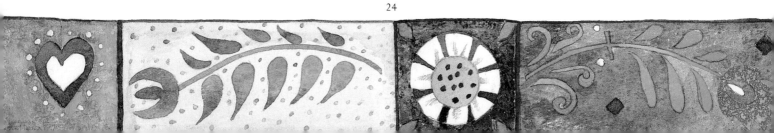

But, especially, you must make my bed each morning, shaking the eiderdown till the feathers fly like snowflakes, so that there will be snow on the earth. It must be so, for I am Mother Holle."

In this way the girl entered into the service of Mother Holle. As the days passed, the old woman was more and more delighted with the girl's help, particularly the way she shook her eiderdown each morning. For she shook it laughingly till clouds of feathers flew up and fell thickly to the ground. And as she worked, she sang:

Shake and fly!

Shake and fly!

Till the feathers rise

And fall from the sky.

The old woman and the girl lived happily together for some time, feasting on the good food cooked by Mother Holle at the end of each busy day. After they had eaten, they would sit outside the house under an elder tree. There they talked and talked as the pollen fell from the white flowers above them, and still they sat there talking when the clusters of red berries hung heavily from the tree, or lay crushed on the path beside them, leaving bright stains.

Then one day, as the girl shook the eiderdown and watched the feathers hesitate in the air before descending, all at once tears filled her eyes and sadness filled her heart. As they feasted together that evening, she shared her unhappiness with Mother Holle, who nodded her head as she listened, seeming to understand this sudden longing for life back above ground. She even seemed pleased by the girl's desire to return. After a moment of quietness, she said, "You have served me well and generously, dear girl. I will be sad to see you go, but go you must. I myself will guide you back to where you belong."

Mother Holle took the hand of the girl and led her to a large door, which she opened and urged her through. Just as the girl entered the doorway, shining flecks of gold fell down on her like a shower of rain. They settled all over her, from head to toe. As the gold-covered maiden stood there in astonishment, Mother Holle handed back to her the lost spindle. "All these gifts are yours," she said. "The spindle you need and the gold you have won." With that the old crone closed the door and the girl found herself on the earth,

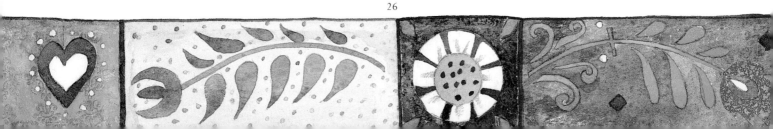

very close to her home. As she passed the well, the old cock recognised her and heralded her homecoming:

Cock-a-doodle-doo!

Your girl's come back to you.

She's lovely, good, and golden too.

Cock-a-doodle-doo!

The girl's stepmother and stepsister rushed out of the house and they were so impressed by the gold that even they welcomed her. When they heard what had happened, they envied her good fortune and immediately started to plan how the lazy daughter might get hold of the same treasure. They plotted late into the night.

Next morning, the second girl went straight to the well to begin the hunt for her fortune. Remembering her stepsister's story, she thrust her hand into a thorn bush to prick her finger, since she hated spinning. Though there was scarcely a speck of blood on the spindle, she threw it purposefully into the well, and without a moment's thought, she threw herself after it, arriving at the bottom even before the spindle. She set off at once to find the oven and the tree, ignoring the sunshine and flowers.

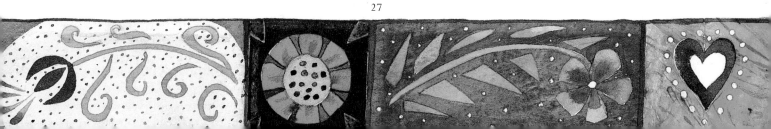

She saw the oven ahead of her and marched right up to it, listening impatiently while the loaves called out to her, "Take us out! Oh, please take us out, or else we will burn. We have been baking long enough!"

The selfish girl drew back from the hot oven, replying, "Why should I get all sweaty and dirty?" She walked on, leaving the bread to burn.

She soon came to the apple tree. But when the apples called out, "Pick us! Oh, please pick us or we will soon be too ripe," she became annoyed.

"Why should I shake you free? I might get hurt." She was anxious to get to the old woman's house, so she pushed past, leaving the tree groaning under its load.

When she arrived at the cottage, she went straight up to the door, heedless of the face at the window. Thinking of her stepsister's experience, she was quite untroubled by the horrible teeth of the old crone who came to the door. "Can I come and stay with you?" she demanded, without so much as a greeting.

She began well, forcing herself to perform the tasks her sister had described. But it was all such a bore and a bother!

On the first day, she made herself shake the eiderdown till some of the feathers flew. On the second day, she lifted it half-heartedly and threw it back on the bed, so that a few, solitary feathers stirred but did not rise. After that, she gave up and slept till noon. Or she would lie in bed thinking where she would hide her gold when she arrived home.

Mother Holle became sad and angry at such behavior and, after some time, she asked the lazy girl to leave. The girl was more than happy to do so, and even ran ahead of the old woman, who hobbled over to the large door. Mother Holle opened it and the girl placed herself under the arch, looking up expectantly.

Imagine her horror when what fell down on her was not golden rain, but

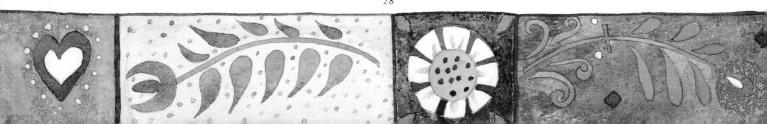

a torrent of thick, black tar. Mother Holle said to her, "This alone is yours. The tar is your reward for your service, but the spindle you have not deserved." Then the door closed firmly against her.

The tarred daughter cried with rage and staggered past the well to her mother's house. But as she passed by, the cock cried out to announce her return:

Cock-a-doodle-doo!

Your girl's come back to you.

She's lazy, mean, and dirty too.

Cock-a-doodle-doo!

VASILISA THE BEAUTIFUL

RUSSIAN

Once upon a time and far away, a merchant lived with his wife and their only child. She was so lovely that they called her Vasilisa the Beautiful. When Vasilisa was eight years old, her mother became very ill. On her deathbed she drew her daughter to her and said: "I must leave you, dear child. And yet I will always be with you. I bless you with this gift of a little doll that I have made for you. You must not let anyone else know about her. Whenever you are in need, she will help you. Feed her well, and she will tell you all you need to know." Both mother and daughter wept and embraced each other, and then the sick woman died.

The merchant soon chose another wife, a widow who had two daughters of her own. Vasilisa was hated by her stepmother and stepsisters because she was so lovely and kind. They were jealous of her right from

the start. They treated her cruelly and gave her all the unpleasant work to do. And yet, no matter how abused and neglected she was, she still grew more and more beautiful, while the stepsisters sat around and got uglier by the day.

Vasilisa's secret support and comfort was, of course, her doll, for whom she saved all the best scraps of food. Each evening she would spread them like a feast for her little companion when they were alone in the attic. She would tell the doll her sorrows and then ask:

Little doll, little doll,

What shall I do?

For I'm lonely and sad

and hungry too.

The doll always consoled her, and she would heal Vasilisa when she was sick, for she knew all the medicinal herbs in the garden.

Life got worse for Vasilisa when her father left home to make a long voyage. While he was away, the family moved to a cottage at the edge of a thick forest. The stepmother knew that at the heart of this wood lived the witch Baba Yaga. Aware of the danger, she often sent Vasilisa into the forest on errands, but her little doll kept Vasilisa from harm.

In the wintertime, one sister had to weave, the other had to knit, and Vasilisa had to do the spinning. They settled down to work one evening by the light of a candle. When the flame began to flicker, one sister pretended to trim the wick but, following a prearranged plan, snuffed it out instead and cried, "We cannot possibly work in the dark! Vasilisa, you will have to go to Baba Yaga's house to get more light."

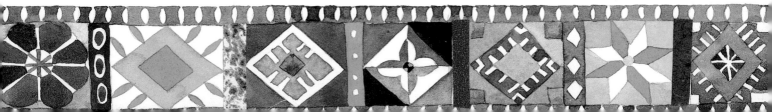

As Vasilisa and her doll set off in the darkness, a strange horseman rode up. He was dressed in white from head to toe and he sat on a milk-white horse with a silver bridle that jangled as the horse shook its mane. As he passed, light began to grow all around them. Then, as they walked deeper into the forest, a horseman all in red rode by—and the sun rose in the sky.

Vasilisa and her doll walked the whole day before reaching the clearing where Baba Yaga's hideous cottage stood. The moment Vasilisa saw it, she felt afraid. The fence and gate were made of bones and the posts were crowned

with skulls. The gate lock was a wide-open mouth edged with sharp teeth.

Suddenly, a third horseman, as black as coal from head to toe, rode up to the house. As soon as he reached the gate, he disappeared, and night fell over the forest. In the gloom, the skulls began to light up, creating an eerie glow. Vasilisa could scarcely breathe for fright. The trees swayed and the branches scratched against each other as Baba Yaga herself arrived in her flying mortar, rowing with her pestle and sweeping her tracks away behind her with her broom. Snuffing at the air with her pointed nose, she screeched, "Some

Russian is here. I smell a strange Russian! Tell me who you are at once!"

Vasilisa stepped out and curtsied before the old hag. "It is Vasilisa, old woman. I have been sent to get light for my stepsisters."

"Aha!" the witch replied. "You may have some light, but only after you have done enough work for me." At the sound of her voice, the doors jumped open, and Vasilisa followed her into the house.

Once inside, the old hag called out, "Bring me food from the oven and beer from the cellar." Vasilisa served her by the light she had fetched from the fearful skulls on the fence posts. Greedily the old hag ate her fill and left hardly anything for the girl. But this Vasilisa put in her apron pocket. When Baba Yaga yawned and got ready to go to bed, she gave Vasilisa these orders: "While I am away tomorrow, make sure that you clean the house properly. Scrub the floors and sweep the yard. Do the washing and make the beds. Prepare my supper and, most importantly, sort the grain from the chaff in my bins. If all is not done well, I shall surely devour you!"

Once Baba Yaga was asleep and the hut was shaking with her snoring, Vasilisa gave her doll the food she had saved and poured out her heart to her. Once again, she was comforted, and then she lay down to sleep. When she awoke, Baba Yaga was already up and ready to leave in the darkness.

The lights in the clearing were only a glimmer when the white horseman suddenly rode by. In the dawn light, the old hag got into her mortar and rowed herself away with her pestle. As she left, the red horseman rode by, and the sun rose. Vasilisa stood in the garden and watched Baba Yaga leave, and by the time she had returned to the house to start her day's chores, she found them already completed. She thanked her doll, who reminded her that supper must still be

prepared. "And after you have done that," she added, "relax and rest."

At the end of the day, Baba Yaga returned with the black horseman. The forest was filled with night and the skulls again glowed in the darkness. The trees swayed and branches scratched as Baba Yaga screamed, "I hope that you have finished your work or I'll surely devour you!"

She sulked when she found that Vasilisa had taken care of everything. All that remained was the grinding of the grain that had been sorted from the chaff. At Baba Yaga's bidding, three pairs of hands appeared from nowhere, performed the task, and carried the flour away.

Once more the old crone ate a huge supper and left barely a scrap for the girl. As she rose from the table she said, "Make sure you work just as hard tomorrow. And, most importantly, you must clean all the poppy seeds one by one, for dirt has fallen in the bin."

Then, as the house shook with Baba Yaga's snoring, Vasilisa gave the doll her food. When she had finished eating, the doll said, "Now say the prayers your mother taught you and sleep in peace till the morning light."

The next day, everything happened as before. When she returned with the black night, Baba Yaga once again gave a command to her mysterious servants, and three pairs of hands appeared from nowhere to press the oil out of

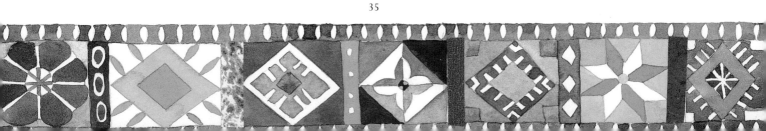

the cleaned poppy seeds. Then the hag ate her huge supper. When she had swallowed a few spoonfuls, she looked up from her soup. "Are you dumb?" she asked Vasilisa abruptly. "Why don't you speak?"

"No, I am not dumb, but I am afraid," the girl replied. "Still, I would like to know the answers to some questions."

Baba Yaga stared at her and said, "Beware, little girl, for it is dangerous to know too much. Remember that."

Despite her fear, Vasilisa went ahead with her questions: "Who is the white horseman, and why does he come?"

"He is my bright daylight," Baba Yaga replied.

"Who is the red horseman, and why does he come?"

"He is my rose-red sunrise," Baba Yaga replied.

"Who is the black horseman, and why does he come?"

"He is my black night," Baba Yaga replied. "They are my mysterious servants," she added.

Vasilisa then remembered the three pairs of hands that had appeared from nowhere and ground the grain and pressed the oil, but she said nothing.

"I do have more questions," Vasilisa offered, "but you said that it was dangerous to know too much." And she was silent again.

Baba Yaga was pleased that she had not pried further and said, "I eat those who are too inquisitive! And now I have a question for you. How have you been able to do all the chores I set for you while I was away? There was far too much for one girl to do on her own."

Vasilisa replied truthfully, "I did it all through my mother's love and blessing."

Baba Yaga was amazed and retorted, "Love and blessing! Get out of my

house with your blessings!" Roughly she pushed Vasilisa out of the hut and gruffly she called out to her, "Take the light you were sent for. And be off!"

So Vasilisa found her way home by the light of the skull, which she carried at the end of a fence post. The house was in darkness as she entered, for her stepsisters could make no candle stay alight while she was gone. "Thank goodness you have brought us light," was all her stepmother could say, and the sisters grabbed the skull from her. But, as they did so, it sent off rays so powerful that it blinded them all. They could not escape the light no matter where they hid and, finally, it consumed them completely.

Vasilisa buried the skull in the earth and left the forest for the town. There she lodged with a kind old woman.

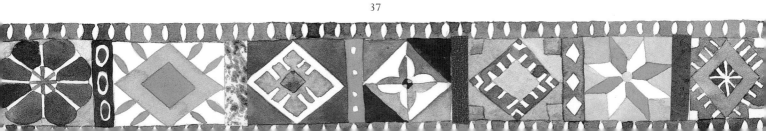

Since she did not want to be idle while she waited for her father's return, Vasilisa began to spin flax, and she produced a thread just like gossamer—so thin that no one could work with it, and too fine for any comb or shuttle. She appealed to her doll who was, as always, willing to help. "Bring me any old shuttle and I will do the weaving," she said.

As Vasilisa slept, the doll worked. She went on weaving throughout the winter, until all the gossamer thread had been woven into exquisite cloth. Vasilisa gave the material to the kind woman who had lodged her, saying, "Take this and sell it, then keep the money for yourself."

But the old woman protested, "This is truly royal cloth. The Tsar himself must have it!"

So saying, she set off for the palace, and would show the cloth only to the Tsar. When he saw it, he desired it at once. The woman insisted that since the cloth was indeed priceless, it could not be purchased, but the Tsar might have it as a gift. He was delighted and immediately ordered shirts to be made. But the fabric was so delicate that no one dared sew it, so he sent for the old woman and asked her if she would make the shirts. When she refused, he said, "But if you made this fine cloth, surely you must be able to sew it?"

"No, I could never make such cloth," the old woman replied. "It is my foster daughter who can spin and weave so finely." So the Tsar then insisted that her foster daughter make his shirts for him.

When Vasilisa heard this, she was not at all surprised and set to work, not stopping until she had finished the garments. Then she combed her hair, put on her best gown and sat at her window, waiting to see what would happen next.

As soon as the old woman returned from the palace after delivering the

shirts, the royal messengers were at her door, proclaiming that the Tsar wanted to thank and reward the one who could make such marvellous garments. So Vasilisa hurried to the palace with her doll in her pocket.

The Tsar loved her at first sight. Taking her hands in his, he said "Vasilisa the Beautiful, I ask you to be my bride. You will be my queen and we will live together in peace." Vasilisa was delighted and went at once to live in the palace, joined by the kind old woman and her father when he returned from his travels. No one ever knew about her mother's gift, which she kept with her forever, and each day she thanked the doll for her good fortune.

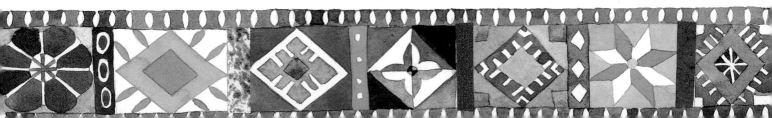

OLD MOTHER SWAN AND GREAT MOTHER EARTHQUAKE

IROQUOIS

In past times there lived a woman who had three grown daughters, Round Stone, Long Legs, and Shaking Leaf. When they were the right age, Mother Swan had to arrange for the girls' marriages, so she called them to her and said, "My life has been very difficult raising you alone. I have worked hard to care for you, living off wild mushrooms and fruit, but now I can no longer provide for you. I am getting old and need to eat some meat if I am to survive another winter. It is time for you to marry into another clan. Two of you will journey to the territory of the Eagle people. There you will find Great Mother Earthquake, who is rich and lives in a large lodge with

her son Scar Face. Mother Earthquake will make a good mother-in-law, and her son is a good hunter who will make a fine husband. Take them the finest bread you can bake, and bring back the best meat you can find for me."

The two older girls, Round Stone and Long Legs, were happy with their mother's plan and immediately began to prepare their marriage bread. They washed the grain and ground the corn; they mixed and kneaded the dough and shaped twenty round loaves; they baked them in the ashes, then packed them in a large basket they wove from pine roots and birch bark. They girls lay down to sleep early, so that they could depart at dawn. Before they left, Mother Swan drew them to her to braid their hair and paint stripes on their faces. As they said goodbye, she spoke firmly: "You must go straight to the lodge of Mother Earthquake. Do not speak to anyone or stop along the way. Remember what I say."

The pair set off with their marriage bread, watched by Shaking Leaf, who was left behind. By afternoon they had forded many cold streams; their moccasins were covered with mud, and their feet were bruised from the sharp rocks. Suddenly, an old man of the Owl people ran in front of them in great distress. "I have lost my arrow shooting at a rabbit," he cried. "I must find it, for I must take meat home to my family. Please help me find my arrow." Long Legs was reluctant to help, for she remembered her mother's instructions, but her older sister Round Stone put down the basket and joined in the search. However, she was tricked—for while she was searching, Owl ran away with the marriage bread.

Sadly, the girls went back home, knowing that their mother would be disappointed. Long Legs explained what had happened and Mother Swan cried, "How could you disobey me? I told you to go straight to the Eagle lodge. Now you have come back without meat." She wept till the sun disappeared behind the trees. Then she said to Long Legs, "Go to sleep, and tomorrow

we will begin again. We will make the marriage bread and you and Shaking Leaf will go find Mother Earthquake and her son. Your older sister must now stay and make the best of it."

Before the sun rose the bread was made. Again, Mother Swan braided her daughters' hair and painted their faces. Again, she said to them, "Do not stop to talk to anybody as your other sister did. Go straight to Mother Earthquake, and do not stray from the path."

The two younger sisters set off determined to do as their mother commanded. But before the sun was high in the sky, the same Owl man appeared on the road, greeting them with smiles. Remembering her sister's fate, Shaking Leaf urged, "Do not stop to talk to him, sister. We must hurry on to find Mother Earthquake."

But Long Legs was won over by Owl's kind manner and she stopped to ask him the way. "Great Mother Earthquake lives very near," he replied. "In fact, you can see her lodge from here." Deceitfully, he pointed to his own lodge, for although he already had a wife and a son, he thought these Swan girls would be beautiful brides.

The cunning fellow ran home ahead of them. He sent his son out, and covered his wife with ashes so that she looked very old. Then he painted himself brightly, so that he looked like a young brave, and he sat down to wait for the girls.

When they saw him in the dim light of the lodge, they assumed that he was their desired husband and sat down with him. But as they talked of their hard journey, a messenger can running in. "Come quickly, Owl, you must come to the lodge. Hurry! Do not keep Mother Earthquake waiting!"

Owl sprang up to leave, afraid to displease the old woman. "I am needed at their council," he pretended. "But I will soon be back. Do not be puzzled.

I am Scar Face and Owl is my nickname." With that he ran off.

Shaking Leaf knew that something was amiss. "This man is a deceiver," she said. "We should not have stopped. But let us now leave quickly." The girls picked up their basket and hurried on their way. When they grew hungry, they stopped to pick berries, since Mother Swan had taught them about all the plants in the wild country. Eventually, they reached Great Mother Earthquake's lodge.

The girls could hear the sound of laughter and dancing. They peeped in through the window to see Owl prancing foolishly to entertain the Eagle people. After his crazy performance, he left the lodge. Quickly, the girls hid behind the trees so that he did not notice them. Then they waited until the other visitors had left, leaving only Mother Earthquake and her son beside the fire.

Long Legs and Shaking Leaf entered the lodge and approached the fire shyly. They put their basket down on the floor in front of Great Mother Earthquake, who smiled kindly, picked up the bread, and gave some to her son. "Scar Face, this bread is brought as a marriage gift. Eat and be married," she said. Scar Face took the bread from his mother and looked curiously at the girls. Then he too smiled. He bowed his head to his mother and ate the bread gift with pleasure, while the two girls sat down, one on each side of him.

After the marriage celebrations, the wives lived with Scar Face and Mother Earthquake. They were very happy with their new life: every day they ate well and in the evenings they listened to the stories of the Eagle people. And so the weeks went by, until one day Mother Earthquake said, "You are now rested and strong. You must go back to your old mother and take her some meat. When she is stronger and able to make the journey, bring her to

live with us here. She can have her own fire, from the wood you gather. She can have her own pot, and cook her own meat for as long as she has teeth."

Then Long Legs and Shaking Leaf packed dried meat in a huge bundle—but before they even tried to lift it, Mother Earthquake touched it and immediately it shrank. It became so small that they could pick it up and carry it with ease. The girls were astonished, but they thought it best not to say anything. Quietly, they left the lodge and made their way back home.

When they laid their meat gift in front of Mother Swan, she was not very impressed, but as soon as she touched the bundle it grew again. She was amazed at the size. "You have done well, my daughters," she said with delight. Her eyes shone and the sweat ran down her cheeks as she sat by the fire chewing on the cooked meat. "Thank you, dear daughters," she exclaimed. Mother Swan was not used to so much chewing, so she was soon exhausted. When she could not possibly eat any more, she lay down and slept the most peaceful sleep she could remember.

When Old Mother Swan felt strong enough, she traveled back to the Eagle people with all her daughters. And so she ended her years, contented beside her own fire in Great Mother Earthquake's lodge, with her daughters and granddaughters safe and prosperous around her.

SNOWFLAKE

SLAVIC

In days gone by in a village in Slavonia there lived a childless couple called Marie and Ivan. They loved each other very much, but their happiness felt empty because they had no children. As they grew old, they found that the delight they had always known when they watched other people's children at play had turned to sadness. "If only we had children of our own," they said to each other, but as the years passed they gave up all hope of having their wish granted.

One cold winter—the coldest anyone could remember—the snow fell for days and lay in deep drifts around the houses in the village. On a bright, crisp morning as Marie and Ivan sat at their window watching the children build snow men and snow women, and listened to their cheerful shouting, a weight suddenly lifted from Ivan's heart and he exclaimed, "Marie, let us go out and build our own snow woman!"

His wife was pleased at the idea. "Yes, that will give us a morning's pleasure," she said. "But instead of making a snow woman, let us make a snow child. Then we can care for her as if she were real. We may not have any children but no one can stop us from making our own snow daughter!" And dressing up warmly in thick boots and coats, hats, and scarves, they went out into the garden.

Marie and Ivan were so excited by their plan that they soon forgot about the cold. They worked with all the strength in their stiff, old bones until they had rolled enough snow to form the body and feet and arms of the snow child. Finally, they placed the snow head on top. Their neighbors were quite surprised to see the old couple toiling and laughing out in the snow. "What are they doing?" they asked each other.

As Marie and Ivan worked on the head and face, gently shaping ears and eyes, nose and mouth, they grew happier and happier. At last, the snow child was finished. Stamping their feet on the icy ground, the couple stepped back to admire the result of their morning's work.

Marie could not resist going closer to the snow child. As gently as she could, she laid her hand on the snow child's cheek and tears pricked her eyes. All of a sudden, she felt a quick, cool breeze. To her astonishment, she realized that it was human breath, coming from the mouth of the snow child. Looking more closely, she found herself gazing into a pair of deep blue eyes that gazed back at her. Slowly, the lips turned strawberry red and began to smile.

Ivan was suddenly afraid. "What have we done?" he cried out, and he nervously crossed himself.

But Marie felt a deep peace in her heart as they watched the awakening girl begin to move her arms and legs, and bend her head and turn it from side to side. "God has sent us this gift," she said as she reached out her arms to embrace the cold snow child. "She is our daughter and her name is Snowflake." Marie kissed and hugged the girl, and as she did so, the snow fell from her, leaving her skin smooth and soft. Joyfully, Marie took her new daughter into the house.

Day by day, Snowflake grew, and as she grew her beauty increased. She was glad and carefree and she brought laughter to the quiet cottage. Marie felt new life in her old fingers and she sewed the most lovely dresses for her child. She baked every morning and the house was filled with the good smells of freshly cooked bread and cakes. The village children came to play with Snowflake in her garden and Marie and Ivan were no longer alone.

Snowflake was kind and good and very clever. She learned things quickly and delighted in the world around her. Her red lips smiled, her blue eyes gleamed, and her golden hair shone in the light. But Marie noticed that her cheeks were always white; they were never rosy like other children's. She saw this and felt a pang in her heart, but she spoke of her fear to no one.

The winter was long and cold, but never had Marie and Ivan been so contented. They looked forward even more to the long days of summer when the children could play long into the evening. At last the days began to lengthen, the trees began to bud, the grass grew green again. As the birds built nests and sang on the branches, the children sang, too, and danced on the village green.

Spring is coming,

We dance in the sun.

Spring is coming,

But how do you come?

Do you blow with the warm wind,

Or ride with the plow?

The spring has come,

We know not how.

But Snowflake did not join in the dancing. Instead she sat quietly watching from the window. Marie saw this and was sad. She put her arm round her child and asked, "Are you sick, dear one? Or have you quarrelled with your friends? Why do you sit here and not go out to welcome the spring?"

But Snowflake could only murmur, "Do not fret, Mother. I am fine."

As spring filled the meadows with golden flowers, and the returning swallows built nests for their new chicks, the children could scarcely remember what cold snow felt like. But Snowflake grew melancholy and began to hide in the shadows, never going out into the sunlight with her playmates. The only thing that relieved her sadness was the shade of the willow tree, where she would lie listening to the stream bubbling by.

Marie herself grew pale as she watched her daughter become more list-less with each passing day. Snowflake no longer went out in the daytime, but only at dusk or in the twilight before dawn. At noon, Marie would find her asleep, curled up in her cool bedroom under the thatch. Every day she seemed to grow thinner and paler.

One day, grey clouds covered the sun, the wind rose, and a fierce storm broke over the village. For a few hours, Snowflake's spirits recovered and she laughed and sang again. But as soon as the sky began to clear and the sun drove the clouds away, her spirits drooped and she wept. Her tears were not warm like the tears of other children. They were as cold as ice.

Summer came and the children prepared to celebrate Midsummer's Day in the woods. The village girls called to Snowflake, "Come and play with us. You must come and play with us! Marie, tell Snowflake to join us in our dancing in the forest."

But Marie's heart ached; she feared what might happen if her daughter ventured out at the height of summer. She knew that her daughter was a child of the snow, and that she needed the chill of winter if she was to become strong and well again. Snowflake was also hesitant, but the girls were so eager for her to come with them that they took her by the hand and pulled her into their circle. Marie kissed her goodbye. "Have fun in the forest, dear one. But do be careful." And to the chil-dren she said, "Take good care of Snowflake. She is the joy of my heart and the light of my life."

The girls ran off to the trees, dancing and running. They picked white-petaled daisies and wreathed them into their hair. The songs they sang were

both happy and sad; they laughed and wept together, and Snowflake tried
to join in their celebrations.

As the sun began to set, the girls gathered dry grasses and twigs to kindle a
fire. When darkness fell, they threw branches on their fire, and gathered round
it. They formed a line, with Snowflake at the very end, and they called out to
her, "Do as we do. Run and jump high over the flames." One by one, they leapt
over the fire to the other side, squealing with delight as they jumped.

Suddenly, in the gloom, they heard a plaintive sigh followed by a sorrowful
groan. The girls looked about and from one to the other, but they could not
tell where the sound came from. Then one of the girls cried out, "Where is

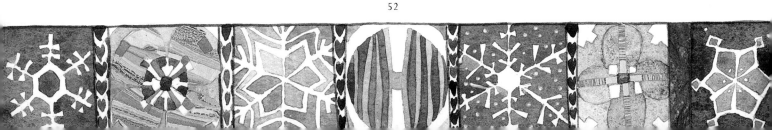

Snowflake? She's not here." They hunted everywhere for her, thinking she was teasing them. "Snowflake!" they called. "Snowflake?" they questioned with growing concern. There was no reply. After more searching, the girls walked slowly back to the village, thinking that their playmate must have gone home alone.

But Snowflake was not at home, and at daybreak the search began again. For days the villagers hunted, calling out, "Snowflake! Where are you? Come back to us." There was never a reply.

Sadly, the children went back to their play. But Marie and Ivan never gave up. "Snowflake, my dearest snow child," Marie would call, "Where are you?" Sometimes she imagined she heard a response, but it was never more than an echo. She went on searching, and went on hoping till the end of her days that her child was not dead, but alive somewhere.

And where had Snowflake gone? She had melted at once when the fire touched her, and only a wisp of mist remained.

THE MOTHER'S MIRROR

JAPANESE

In a remote region of Japan, far away from all the cities, there once lived a husband and wife made very happy by the birth of a daughter. They called her Sachiko, and she was a very happy child. As she passed through her childhood, her life was celebrated at every stage with the ritual gift that accompanied each one: her first kimono, then its broad sash, and, of course, her set of dolls for the annual doll festival.

One day, when Sachiko was about seven years old, she was separated from her father for the very first time, for he had to travel to a city many days' journey from home. In his absence, mother and daughter lived as contentedly as they might, enjoying their days together but wishing for the father's return. When eventually he did come home, worn out by his long journey, he could not sleep until he had given his wife and daughter the gifts

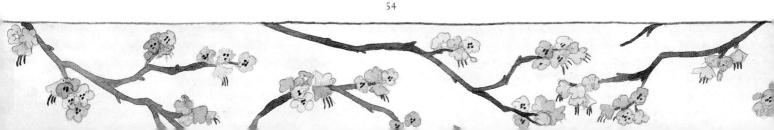

he had brought back for them. Sachiko hung on to his long sleeves and would not let go until he searched deep in his big basket for her present.

The little girl trembled as she took the parcel from him and began to unwrap it. She was delighted when she found a beautiful painted box of candy and an exquisite little doll, wearing a kimono just like her own. She bowed before her father and thanked him from the bottom of her heart. Then she watched her mother receive her gift from the city.

At first, they did not know what it was, for they had never seen a mirror before. Her mother was enchanted as she looked into the glass and saw smiling back at her a most lovely lady, wearing a kimono the color of the sky, just like her own. Her husband, who had begun to know something of the ways of the city, kept explaining to mother and daughter how the mirror worked, but they remained both bewildered and delighted with its magic. He told them that a woman's mirror was said to be a reflection of her heart, and that the mirror must be kept clean and sparkling.

Sachiko's mother enjoyed the mirror for months, taking pleasure in its image. Then one day she put it away and it was forgotten.

By the time Sachiko was sixteen, she had grown just like her mother in face and in character. She was kind and beautiful, though she was not aware of it. Then, one sorrowful day, her mother became ill. She did not recover, but faded away until she had little strength left. When she knew her last days were approaching, she spoke lovingly to her Sachiko about the future and told her to fetch the mirror from its hiding place. "When I am dead, you must keep this mirror with you always," she said in a feeble voice. "Look into its depths each morning and each evening, and there you will see me smiling

back at you. I will be with you in good times and when you are troubled."
Once she had said this, she could die in peace.

Sachiko, now a young woman, did as her mother bid her every morning
and every evening. There, in the deep mirror, she always saw her mother, not
as she was when she was weak and dying, but as she must have been when
she was young and vital, like herself. Whenever she met the lovely face in the
glass, she was comforted, and so she never felt alone. This remained true
even after her father remarried.

The new wife had cast a spell on Sachiko's father to win his love. The
woman treated Sachiko cruelly, for she was jealous of the tender love the
father showed for his daughter. She looked for any opportunity to make the

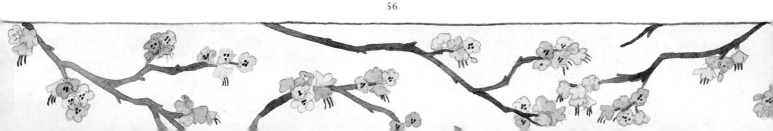

girl suffer, though Sachiko always tried to please her father's new wife, to honor and respect her as she should. It made no difference, however, and Sachiko suffered even more malicious treatment. But each day she took out the mirror and told her mother of the cruelty she had to endure, and always her mother sustained and encouraged her.

The stepmother began to complain to the father about the girl's behavior, but he would hear no ill of her. Jealousy made his new wife suspicious, and finally she came to her husband with a terrible story. "Your young daughter hates me, and I know that she has made an image of me, to which she speaks, cursing me so I will die." She had heard Sachiko speaking with her mirror, but did not know what it was.

She was so distressed that her husband realized that he had to speak of the matter to his daughter. When he came to her room, Sachiko quickly hid the mirror in the sleeve of her kimono, for she wished to keep it to herself. This made her seem guilty, and her father was heartbroken to think that perhaps the charge was true. "What are you hiding from me?" he demanded. "Your stepmother tells me that you have made an image of her and that you are cursing it, in the hope that she will die. Is it true? How could you do such an evil thing?" he cried.

Sachiko was speechless. When he had finished, she replied through her tears, "How could you believe such a thing? When I speak as you describe, I am talking with my mother."

Then she had to tell her secret about the mirror and her mother's last words. Quietly, she pulled the mirror out from the sleeve of her kimono for her father to see—and remember.

Her father recognized the mirror and was full of remorse at her story, to hear how much she grieved the loss of her mother, and how much she had suffered at the hands of her stepmother. He was also pleased to learn how much she was comforted by her mother and the mirror. He wept, and praised Sachiko for her patience and love.

The suspicious stepmother had been listening through the door and heard what passed between them. She too was moved to tears when she realized how much Sachiko had suffered, both from her loss and from the unkind treatment she had received, even when she was trying to please. She was amazed to hear of the mirror and the comfort it brought to the grieving daughter, while she had supposed that the voice she heard was weaving evil

spells. Unable to bear it any longer, she rushed into the room, falling on her knees before the daughter she had wronged.

"I am ashamed. I beg you to forgive me," she cried. "I acknowledge the evil I have done and, in the future, I will try to love you as my own child." The kind girl forgave her at once and they embraced. Then and there, they began a new and happy life.

The family lived contentedly together until Sachiko herself married. Then the day came when she too became a mother, and the day came when she too grew weak and died. But before she died, she gave her daughter the mirror that she had received from her mother, so that her own child could also enjoy her mother's presence and consolation.

KATANYA

TURKISH

In the poorest part of Turkey, a long time ago, there lived a woman who was very poor. She had longed for a child, and the death of her husband did not put an end to this longing. She often prayed to God, yet her prayer was not fulfilled.

But God had seen her love and knew of her heart's desire, so he called his prophet Elijah to him and said, "My faithful messenger, go down to earth for me and visit this lonely woman, and help her."

Elijah was used to such requests. He often appeared to God's people when they were in trouble, and worked miracles with God's power. He came to earth happily to do the Lord's bidding and found the poor old woman in a busy market place.

She was hungry and weak. She had sold everything she had in order to

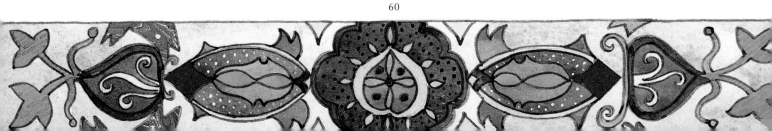

survive from day to day, and now she had nothing left to sell. Each day she visited the market to ask if any of the merchants could let her have just a little of their abundant supplies, perhaps just one apple or a cabbage, or even a single grape. She never got much, but she rarely received nothing.

That day when she reached the market, she found all the merchants muttering, for their taxes had been raised and anyone who had any money was going to have to pay more to the king. This did not affect the poor woman, of course, but the angry merchants were much less kind to her that day and ignored her pleas for help. So she left the market with her stomach empty and her heart heavy.

Then, on the edge of the market place, she noticed a new merchant, quite ragged in his dress and with very little at his stall. In fact, all that she saw was a cluster of six dates, no more. "He's almost as poor as I am," she thought, as she went past him. But, all the same, she could not resist asking, "Please could you let me have just one of those dates? I am very hungry."

The ragged merchant did not hesitate for one moment, but answered kindly, "Yes, of course. Take all you need." The old woman was most grateful and looked hard at the dates, trying to decide which of the six she would choose.

Finally, she picked a very large one, wrapped it in her handkerchief and set off home, with the words, "Thank you for your mercy. May God bless you.'

Back at home, the sun shone brightly through her window and, when the date caught the light, it seemed to glow inside. So she put it near the window, where it lay gleaming in the sunlight. She could not bear to eat it, despite her hunger. So she went back out into the streets to search for some other scrap of food.

While she was away, the sun blessed the date with its power and it began to quicken and then to swell, till finally it burst open. Out jumped a tiny young girl, as small as your little finger, as beautiful as the early morning sun, and clothed in a dress of many colors, as fresh as a rainbow. Looking around her, she noticed to her dismay the poverty of the room and cried out, "How dirty it is here! I must do something about it." It was indeed dirty, for the old woman had exchanged her broom for half a loaf of bread.

The tiny girl jumped through the window and made herself a broom from bits of twigs and straw. Back in the house, she swept the kitchen, making it cleaner than it had ever been, for her little broom could get right into the corners and into every crevice between the floorboards.

Meanwhile, the old woman was making her way home, still hungry and thirsty, when she again met the ragged merchant from the market place. He greeted her and offered her a bald and gleaming olive from his basket. "Good day, kind woman," he said. "Here is a gift for your hunger." She took the olive eagerly and thanked the tattered old man for his pity.

This time, she could not wait till she got home. She bit into the olive there and then. She was very surprised when her teeth felt the hard stone and she took it out of her mouth. It was not an olive stone, but a thick gold coin! "I must give this treasure back to the old man," she thought, and turned round to find him. But though she hunted everywhere, he was not to be found. So she held the gold tightly in her hand and sang with joy all the way home.

Further surprises awaited her there, for instead of dirt she found a clean and sparkling kitchen. "Who could have cleaned my house for me?" she cried out in amazement.

"It is me," said a little voice shyly, "I am your child and I have come to be with you, Mother."

The old woman turned around and around, trying to see where the voice came from. "Here I am, on the window sill," the little voice shouted merrily. And there she was! The old woman could not believe her eyes when she saw such an exquisite small creature laughing up at her. "Kiss me, Mother, for I am your new daughter," said the tiny girl.

So the old woman lifted her with care to her cheek and kissed her gently. She wept as she realized that the date must have been the gift of the prophet Elijah. No one else could perform such joyful magic, she thought.

Since the girl had no name, her new mother said, "I will call you Katanya, for you are my little one."

So began their happy life together. The woman used the gold coin to buy new furniture for the bare cottage, and she stocked the pantry with food. The two of them visited the marketplace and rewarded all the merchants who had been generous when the woman was destitute. But, best of all, the old woman's house rang with Katanya's laughter and singing.

Her foster mother gave Katanya all she needed and made many little dresses for her, though Katanya loved most the many-colored dress that shone like a sparkling rainbow.

Then, one day, a prince rode by her window, on his way home from an unsuccessful search for a bride. As her song penetrated his heart, he fell in love. "I must marry the singer of that song," he vowed.

When the king heard of his son's desire, he sent a messenger to summon the girl and her mother to the palace. So that they might appear suitably

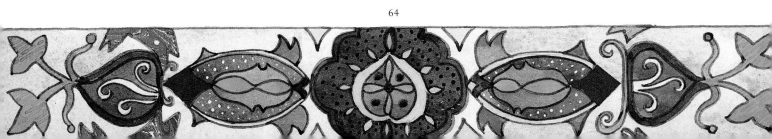

dressed, he also sent the queen's seamstress, to make them new clothes. The old woman gratefully accepted but Katanya refused such fine clothing. "No thank you," she said politely. "I have my own gown. It is the color of rainbows in the sunlight. It will please the prince."

At the appointed time, the old woman in her new gown and Katanya in her rainbow dress went to the palace. At first the people of the court were greatly disappointed, for the mother seemed to have come alone. The prince was sad and asked, "Why have you not brought the singer of my song?"

Then a beautiful, clear voice called out from the woman's pocket, "Here I am!" and Katanya jumped out like a glittering rainbow, singing the same song that had affected the prince so deeply.

"Yes, you are the bride I must marry!" he exclaimed. "Please sing again." So she sang another song, even more lovely than the first.

The marriage took place amid great feasting. Princess Katanya wore her rainbow dress and all were amazed at her pluck and beauty. Her mother came to spend her remaining years in the palace. The prince and his princess lived together in great contentment and God smiled at the work of his servant Elijah.

THE GIRL AND HER GODMOTHER

NORWEGIAN

A very long time ago, a poor man and woman lived quite alone in the depths of a great Norwegian forest. They were so poor that they could not even afford to pay the necessary offering to the priest for the christening when their daughter was born. The father had to make a long journey to the village to try to find a godmother who would pay the offering.

Wearily, he made his way home at the end of the day, having found no one who would stand for his child. Then, as he drew near to his cottage, a beautiful woman approached him, dressed in rich robes and smiling kindly. "I know your errand," she said. "Be content. I will take care of the christening, but after that I must take the child and care for her myself."

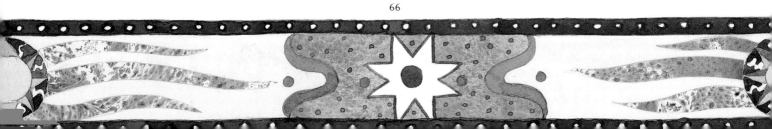

The woodcutter was much relieved by her kindness, but said that he must consult his wife first. So they parted.

His wife would hear nothing of such a deal. "No, no. You must try again tomorrow. This fine lady cannot have our child!"

So the woodcutter went again to another village and searched for a god-mother. But though many were willing, none could afford the offering. Once more he went home sadly and once more the rich woman met him on his path. She was so gentle and generous that he felt sure she would take good care of the girl, and provide for her in a way that they could not, being so poor.

This time, his wife relented a little. "You must try at least one more time to find a godmother for the little one. If you fail, then this fine lady must have our child."

Yet again her husband searched and yet again he was disappointed. No one could afford the offering.

On his return, the rich woman was waiting for him and this time they agreed that she would provide for the christening and then take his daughter away with her. So the girl went to live with her godmother in a large and splendid house, where she was cared for with love and given everything she needed.

When she was about seven years old, her kind godmother explained that she must go on a long journey. "You will stay here while I am away," she said. "You may go where you please in this big house, only you must not enter these three forbidden rooms." She showed her which the forbidden rooms were and then departed.

No sooner had she gone but the little girl became intensely curious and decided that she would open the door to the first room just a crack so that

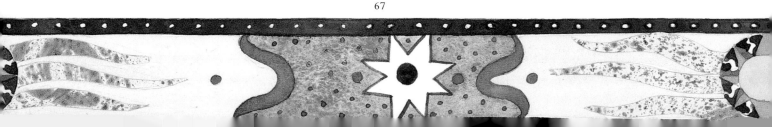

she could see what was in there. But as soon as she did so, a star slid through the crack, and she could not get it back into the room again.

When her godmother returned, she knew at once what had happened. "Since you have lost my star, you must leave here," she said angrily. But the girl was upset and wept so much that she relented and they lived together happily again.

The day came when the godmother must go on another journey. She reminded the girl that two rooms were forbidden her, but that all the others she may freely enter. As soon as the child was alone, curiosity overcame her as it had before and she declared, "This time I will be more careful, and just

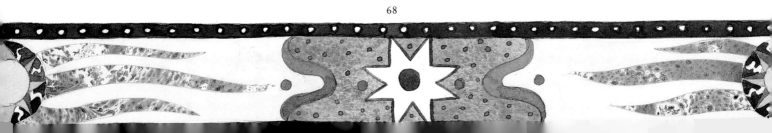

open the door a tiny bit." But no sooner had she turned the knob than the moon slipped out and she could not put it back. "Oh dear, what shall I do?" she moaned. "Now I certainly will be sent away for my disobedience!"

When her godmother returned and discovered the missing moon, she was even angrier than before and threatened to send her godchild away. But once more the girl wept and pleaded and was allowed to remain.

The two of them lived on contentedly for some time, but eventually her godmother again had to travel away from home. She was even clearer this time about the last forbidden room and urged her goddaughter to be obedient. "I will surely obey this time," the girl resolved as she waved her

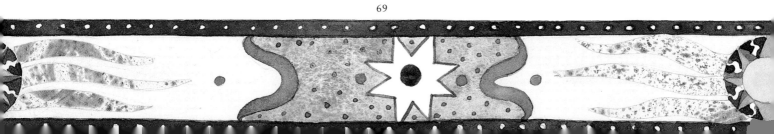

godmother goodbye. Yet no sooner was she alone than she felt she must go to the third room. "Just the tiniest crack this time," she thought—but it was not possible. Before she knew it, the sun burst through the door.

This time she could not escape punishment, despite her pleading. With a sad heart, her godmother said she must leave. "However, you may have one choice before you set off on your own into the world. You may choose either to be the most beautiful woman in the world, but without speech, or you may have the power of speech, but be the ugliest of women. Make your choice."

The girl replied, "I would rather be beautiful," and at once her speech left her and her beauty increased until it was amazing to behold.

They wept as they parted and the girl made her way into the dense forest. As night drew near, she grew afraid and found a tree beside a pool where she could shelter safely for the night. At first light, a servant girl came from a palace nearby to fetch water for the prince who lived there. As she bent over the pool to fill her pitcher, she caught sight of the reflection of the girl up in the tree, looking down from above.

The servant mistook the lovely face for her own and cried out, "I had no idea that I was so beautiful. I should not be a servant fetching water!" She threw down her pitcher and ran back to the castle.

The next morning, another servant girl came to get water, and she too saw the loveliest of faces and mistook it for her own. "Such a beauty should do more than haul water," she cried, and ran back to the castle.

When the prince heard this story, he was curious, and he went at dawn to the same pool. When he saw the lovely face, he knew it could not be his own,

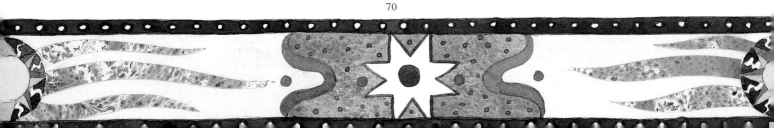

and he gazed into it in amazement. Then he looked up at the girl in the tree and persuaded her to come down to him and return with him to the castle. Though she could not speak, he loved her and invited her to be his bride.

So they were married, although the prince's mother did not share their joy. "She's probably a witch," the queen exclaimed, "for she cannot even speak." But the prince loved her all the more.

When their first child was born, they were delighted. But in the deep sleep that follows birth, the godmother appeared, cut the baby's finger and stained the goddaughter's lips with the blood, saying, "Now you too will know sorrow such as I felt when you lost my star." Then she disappeared with the baby.

The jealous queen said to her son, "I told you so. You have married an ogress who devours her own children." But the prince knew it was not so. He loved and trusted his young wife and he was determined to protect her, so he placed a strong guard about his princess.

When the second baby was born, the godmother again appeared during the sleep that follows birth, and again stained the new mother's lips with blood from the baby's finger, saying, "Now you too will know the sorrow I felt when you lost the moon." Again she disappeared with the baby and again the queen accused the

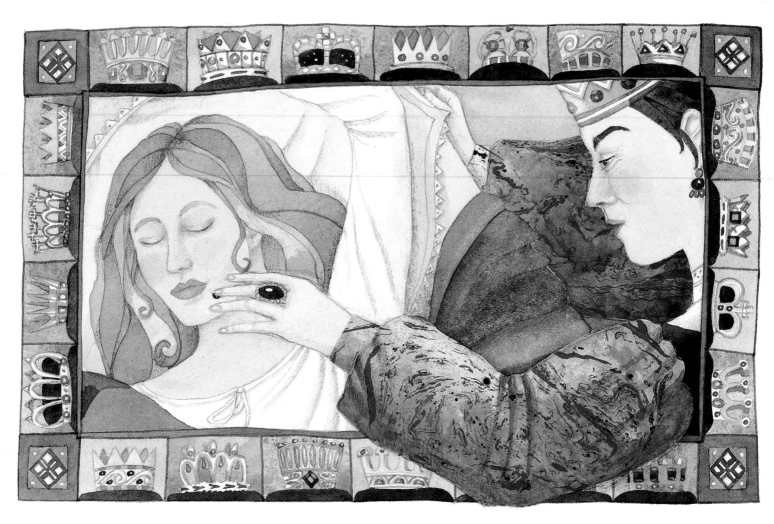

princess of being an ogress. The prince knew it was not so and he placed an even
stronger guard around his wife when the third baby was to be born.

But it was no use; once again the godmother came during the deep sleep
that follows birth and for a third time she cut the baby's finger and smeared
blood round the mother's lips. "Now you will know sorrow such as I felt
when you lost the sun," she said. Once more, she disappeared with the baby.

This time, the prince could not save his wife from punishment. His
mother insisted that she be killed before any more innocent babies lost
their lives. Unable to defend herself, the girl was condemned to die in the
fire as an ogress. But when she was being taken to her execution, the

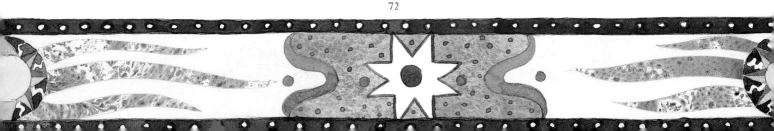

godmother appeared in full sight of everyone, carrying the newest baby in her arms and followed by the other two children. She approached the princess lovingly and placed the baby in her arms, saying, "My dear daughter, here are your children. You must love and care for them now. I am the Queen of Heaven and I have taken all of your children from you so that you might feel suffering, such suffering as I endured when you lost the star and the moon and the sun. Now you understand suffering. Now you may speak." With that she embraced her goddaughter and went on her way.

The prince and princess were overjoyed to recover their children, and since the goddaughter had recovered her speech, she could sing to them all too. Even the queen relented and they all lived together peacefully for many years.

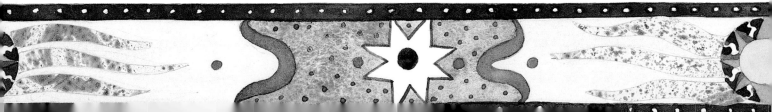

NAOMI AND RUTH

HEBREW

Long, long ago, famine took hold of the land of Judah, and Elimelech with his wife, Naomi, and his two sons left their town of Bethlehem and travelled a long way south to live in Moab. There the man died, and there the sons took wives. But very soon the two sons died too, and Naomi grieved at the loss of husband and sons. She decided to return to Bethlehem, for the famine had passed. So she said to her daughters-in-law, Ruth and Orpah, "Your husbands are dead; now you must go back to your mothers."

The daughters wept and at first refused to leave their mother-in-law. But Naomi insisted and finally Orpah agreed to return to her mother. Sorrowfully they parted. Yet Ruth stood firm, for she loved her mother-in-law dearly. "How can a woman of her age cope on the long hot road back to Bethlehem?" she wondered. So she said to Naomi, "Dear Mother, I will not

leave you. Wherever you go, I will go also and wherever you choose to dwell, I will dwell there with you. Your people will be my people and I will worship your God. I will die in the land where you die, and nothing but death will part us."

Naomi then relented and together they began their journey out from the land of Moab.

On the dusty road, Naomi spoke of the hope she had felt when she left Bethlehem on this road many years before. "My name means 'beautiful'," she said, "but I should now be called Mara, or Bitterness, for so much grief has befallen me. When I left Judah I had a husband and two sons. Now all of them are dead and I have only you to comfort me."

When they reached Bethlehem, the harvest was just beginning. The two women were tired and hungry, so Ruth said, "You stay and rest while I go into the fields to see whether I can glean some barley grain." So she went out, not knowing that the fields belonged to a very rich farmer called Boaz, who was a member of Elimelech's family.

In the evening, Boaz saw a sad young woman gleaning in his fields and asked who she was. One of his workers told him that she was Ruth the Moabite who had accompanied Naomi back to the land of Judah. When he heard that she had followed the reapers all day, gleaning what they had missed, his heart was touched, and he sent for her and said, "You may stay in my fields and take what you like, and you may share the food and water that I provide for my reapers.'

Ruth was amazed but puzzled that he should treat her so kindly. Then he explained that he had heard about her devotion to her mother-in-law

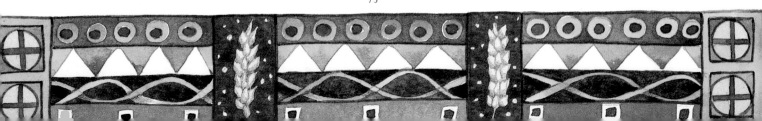

and he marveled that she had left her own people and had come as a stranger to the land of Judah.

So Ruth worked in Boaz's fields. He told his workers to leave plenty of grain for her, so that she could gather enough for the two women to make bread. When Naomi heard Ruth's story, she rejoiced that such kindness should come from her dead husband's kinsman. Ruth went out to the fields every day till the end of the harvest.

When the threshing began, Boaz himself worked on the threshing floor by day, and by night he slept among the sheaves. Naomi had a plan, and she instructed her daughter-in-law, "When night comes, you must also sleep among the sheaves. Lie down near to Boaz." Ruth did as Naomi told her to do, and during the night, when Boaz awoke from disturbed sleep, he was comforted to find Ruth near to him. In the morning, he gave her a sack full of threshed grain. "You must take this back to Naomi," he said.

Day by day, Boaz grew to love Ruth and finally he married her, providing also for her mother-in-law.

Some time later, Ruth rejoiced at the birth of a son. Naomi also rejoiced and her neighbors said to her, "Naomi, God has blessed you richly, for you now have a grandchild. But you are even more blessed in having such a daughter-in-law, who has been kinder to you than seven sons." So Ruth and Naomi lived peacefully together with Boaz, and their family continued to thrive for many generations.

NOTES

In these stories, many recurrent themes illuminate the mother/daughter relationship. Some of the most significant motifs are discussed here.

WOMEN AND NATURE

In myths and fairy tales, women are associated with nature, affirming the earth and the rhythms of life. This can be seen in "Demeter and Persephone"; the goddess and her daughter establish the seasons, enabling life to prevail over death through a repeating cycle of renewal.

Work is very important as a way of interacting with nature. If Mother Holle's bed is not shaken, snow will not fall. Such tasks involve both power and responsibility, symbolizing the energy of creation and the continuing work of nature to maintain life.

Women are friends to the soil, sometimes moving between surface and underground, or even the Underworld. Long Hair pulls a turnip out of the earth to release water imprisoned by the male Mountain spirit. Persephone uproots flowers, opening a hole that leads to Hades. Similarly, it is in the depths of the earth that the feminine must find its fullness in "Mother Holle." The earth is Mother, and girls must be introduced to her mysteries.

The feminine is explored through plant life. Girls like Persephone are associated with flowers, fruits and berries, olives, and ripe apples asking to be picked. They are linked to corn and fertility. This alliance with growth equips women and girls to survive in the wild; Mother Swan and her daughters provide for themselves, as do other girls who are cast out into forest or field.

WOMEN AND HOUSE-KEEPING

"Keeping" here maintains its original senses of tending and celebrating. This attitude toward the home is necessary for sustaining life, and in folktales carries no negative implications of domestic burden. Young girls learn to prepare bread and to take it out of the womb-like oven when it is baked. Those who refuse this symbolic task, like the second girl in "Mother Holle," are denied genuine initiation into womanhood.

Folktale women are often found in the kitchen because that was the emotional center of the home, the place of fire, feeling, and transformation. Raw food is cooked there, skill and care transforming mere sustinence into something comforting and delicious. It is a place of culture.

These symbols associate the feminine with "resource." Ruth's gleaning, for example, shows how a woman's internal resources can make the most of scarce external provisions; she herself is the real source of abundance. This ability to make much of little is the power of Mother Earthquake, who can make the meat supply large or small. Like the old widow's single olive in "Katanya," the seed is the small source of expanding life. Mothers must prepare their daughters to value the seed, the promise of life.

78

One intriguing household task girls are assigned is the sorting of seeds, a time-consuming process that helps develop discrimination, especially necessary in the realm of feeling. Though compassion is valued, pity must sometimes be denied, as Round Stone learned from the tricky Owl on her journey to Mother Earthquake.

Spinning and sewing symbolize more than economic independence. Spinning is a creative act. The spinning of fairy tales was the gift of women, the first tellers, who spun "yarns" as they spun thread. Spinning also connects women with the thread of life; in Greek mythology, the Fates spin, weave, and cut that thread of every mortal life. Girls like Vasilisa participate in this mystery by making miraculous cloth and sewing royal shirts.

TRUE AND FALSE MOTHERS

The true mother is in tune with the miracle of life. She creates and sustains life through her desire for it — desire for a mate, and desire for a child. Even if she cannot bear children, a woman can be a true mother; both Snowflake and Katanya fulfill a barren woman's desire. The good mother is nurturing and constant. Protecting life is her task, for as long as she is needed; then she must release her daughter from her care, as do the Norwegian godmother and Mother Holle. Demeter is less willing to let go. Mother Swan ensures that her daughters will be under the protection of another true mother when she grows too weak.

The false mother sometimes appears with the loss of a true mother. Such loss is felt as a cruel abandonment and inspires a negative image of "mother," symbolized by the notorious stepmother, who is often accompanied by her own envious daughters. Evil stepmothers thrive where the father is weak or absent. The false mother must be either destroyed ("Vasilisa") or transformed ("The Mother's Mirror") so that the daughter can move forward.

WITCHES AND GODDESSES

The aged crone or witch is a potent and fearsome figure. In a benign and human form, she is represented by Great Mother Earthquake, who carries the wisdom of her clan and rules domestic life. Such witch figures as Mother Holle or Baba Yaga represent primitive forces of nature acting in positive and/or negative ways—ruthless even when kind, punishing those who refuse life, watching over growth.

The "goddess-mother," represented by the Norwegian godmother, contrasts with the earth-dwelling Mother Holle. The godmother is not an actual goddess, but carries similar energy, compensating for the spiritual poverty of the girl's birth mother; she is needed to ensure that soul is developed as well as body.

The goddess Demeter is a mother of superhuman force. The intensity of her love is both nurturing and terrifying, protective and merciless. Her rage at the loss of her child makes her destroy all she has created.

THE COMMUNITY OF WOMEN

Energy is constantly renewed among women. Adult women give life to daughters who mature and in turn put their energy at the service of weakening elders. Long Hair fetches water for her aging mother;

Katanya sweeps for her old foster mother; the first girl to visit Mother Holle shakes out the old woman's eiderdown. This cycle also unites Mother Swan and her daughters, and Ruth and Naomi.

All these tales illuminate the solidarity of women, very often in the absence of men, who go off hunting, working, or fighting away from home. We see how women develop practical and emotional self-sufficiency. It is interesting to note that in these communities, widows and orphans are never devalued; in folktales, figures often judged to be impotent or inferior are frequently the ones to whom treasure comes.

GROWING UP

A necessary part of growing up is separation from the mother, complicated for girls because they must stay connected to their feminine origins. Leaving a good mother is difficult, but necessary; mothers must die eventually, and daughters must be able to live full lives without them. When mothers in these stories die, they often leave their presence with their daughters, especially important if the daughter is still very young (a common fairy tale motif). Sachiko's mirror and Vasilisa's doll sustain the love and power of the mother, ensuring that the daughter will be able to grow healthily in the mother's absence.

Disobedience and curiosity are two vital means by which girls to develop. There is a figure like Eve in most mythologies, and healthy girls share her inclination to find out more than they are told. Forbidden rooms or commands not to stray from the path invite disobedience. Curiosity and the will to become independent are positive impulses in folklore, which depicts subversive daughters who are full of desire, wanting to see and discover and grow.

The journey is intrinsic to fairy tales. We see daughters from all cultures embark on the same course: the passage from girl to woman, from life to death. The journey is a universal symbol of change, regressive and progressive. Daughters risk passage into the forest, over the fire, across country, even underground—all encounters with the unknown. Daughters must learn to face the new and the unfamiliar, for each has a mysterious path.

IN CONCLUSION

These stories explore themes universal to the mother/daughter experience. They reflect what it is to be a natural and spiritual woman; to be in the home and alone in the wild; to distinguish the false from the true; to honor the processes of birth and death. All these must be incorporated into the celebration of life that mothers need to share with their daughters. This is the wisdom that women must pass on, and in all cultures, they do so through the medium of the story.